FIRE

FIRE

by Gail Kay Haines
pictures by
Jacqueline Chwast

William Morrow and Company
New York 1975

1 2 3 4 5 79 78 77 76 75

Library of Congress Cataloging in Publication Data

Haines, Gail Kay.
    Fire.

    SUMMARY: A brief introduction to the characteristics
and uses of fire.
    1. Fire — Juvenile literature. [1. Fire]
I. Chwast, Jacqueline, illus. II. Title.
QD516.H23   541'.361   74-13396
ISBN 0-688-22009-6
ISBN 0-688-32009-0 (lib. bdg.)

Orange and yellow flames leap from a campfire.
Soft blue fire burns gas in a stove.
Circus dogs leap through hoops of flaming red.
Fires can be many beautiful colors.
But fire is not just pretty; it is useful, too.

People have been using fire
for a very long time.
More than 200,000 years ago,
men and women began cooking their food,
warming their caves,
and lighting the dark with fire.

They may have found fire
when lightning struck a tree in the woods.
They brought fire home
and tended it carefully,
keeping it burning
as long as they could.

Later people learned ways to make fire.
They learned how to rub or twirl pieces of w
until the wood became hot enough to burn.
They found that a hard, gray rock called "flint"
could make sparks of fire
when it was banged against metal.

Early people found many uses for fire.
Fire scared away bears and tigers.
It baked clay into bricks and pots.
Fire even shaped metal into tools and weapons.

But the people who lived long ago
did not understand fire.
They thought it was a kind of magic.

Much later scientists began to study fire.
They found that fire happens
when a material called "fuel"
and a gas in the air called "oxygen"
mix together quickly, or combine.

Fuel is like food for a fire.
It can be many different things.
Wood and paper, coal and natural gas
are kinds of fuel.
Anything that will burn
can be fuel for a fire.
These materials are called "flammable,"
which means they can burn.

Oxygen helps fuel burn.
It is a part of the air around us.
We take oxygen from the air into our body
when we breathe.
Using oxygen is like breathing for a fire.

Fire is fuel and oxygen
doing something to each other.
Scientists call this something
a "chemical reaction."

But fuel and oxygen cannot combine by themselves.
They need heat to make the chemical reaction happen.
Even though fire, itself, is hot,
it cannot get started, nor can it keep burning, without heat.

You can do a simple experiment
to show how fire uses fuel, oxygen, and heat.
Ask a parent or teacher to help,
because fire can be very dangerous
if it is not handled carefully.
You will need a candle, a big glass jar, and some matches.

The wax in the candle is fuel.
Heat from a burning match melts some wax
and brings it up through the wick into the air.
When heated wax combines with oxygen in the air,
the candle catches fire.

What happens if you take heat, oxygen, or fuel away?

Blow on the candle.
Blowing puts out the fire
by taking away its heat.

Hold the glass jar upside down
over the burning candle.
Soon the fire uses up all the oxygen in the jar.
Without oxygen, fire goes out.

You can let the candle burn
until all the wax is gone.
When there is no more fuel, fire goes out.

Firemen use these same three ways
to put out large fires.
They pour on water with hoses to wash away heat.
They spray on special foam to shut out the oxygen.
They chop down trees or shut off gas lines
to take away fuel.

As a fire burns,
it uses up fuel and oxygen.
Burning changes them
into other things.

Touch the jar to the candle flame,
and the jar turns black.
Rub the jar with your finger,
and black powder comes off on it.
This powder is made up of tiny bits of the candle
that did not burn all the way.
They have been changed into what is called "carbon."

Hold the glass jar upside down over the flame again.
Soon the jar gets cloudy inside.
If you rub your finger along the cloudy part, it feels wet.
Part of the fuel and oxygen
have been changed into water.

Smoke from a candle
is made of water and carbon
and a gas you cannot see.
This gas is called "carbon dioxide."
Carbon dioxide is the same gas
we blow out of our body when we breathe.
Just like people, a fire takes in oxygen
and gives off carbon dioxide.

Hold your hand near the flame,
but do not touch it.
It feels hot.
When fuel and oxygen burn, they make heat.

Making heat is the most important thing
that a fire does.
Heat is a kind of energy.
Energy is anything that can do work.
Energy can make things move.

When a fire boils water,
the water changes into steam.
Steam has heat energy.
With this energy,
steam can push a piston back and forth
inside an engine.
Steam engines can turn the wheels
to make a locomotive move.

steam

water

Heat energy is sometimes used
to make electricity.
Steam pushes the big generator wheels
that produce electricity.

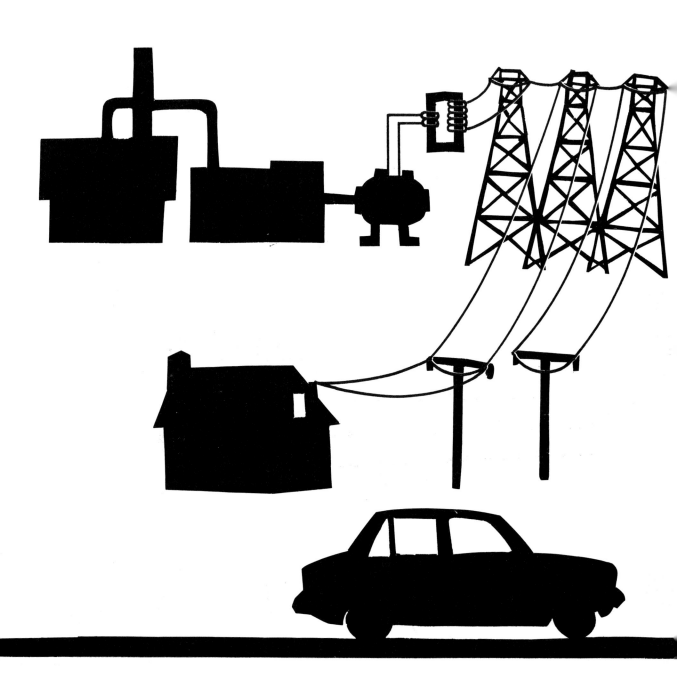

Automobiles could not run without fire's heat.
Gasoline and oxygen burn inside a car's engine.
Heat energy moves pistons up and down
to make the engine work.

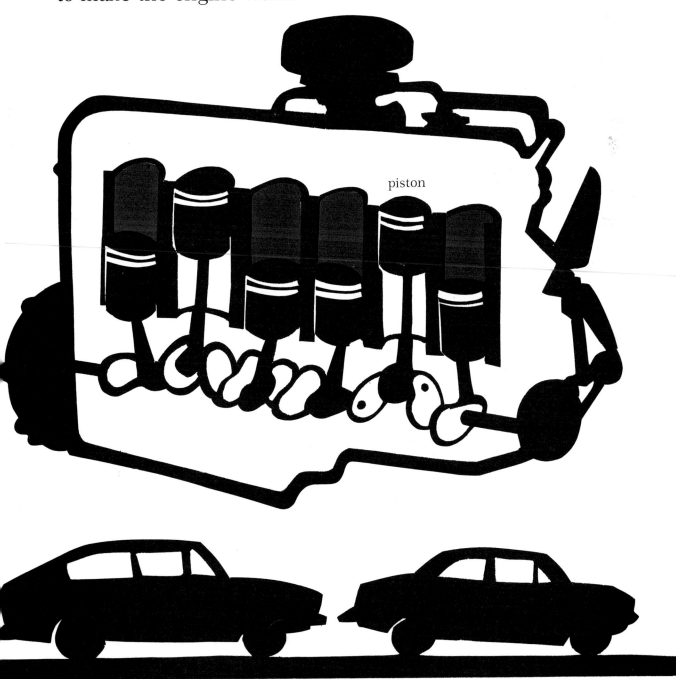

piston

Heat melts and cooks the rubber to make tires.
It helps burn carbon out of iron,
turning the hot, molten iron into steel.
Heat is needed to make cloth and paper and plastic
and just about everything.

Fire in a stove can cook your food.

Fire in a furnace keeps you warm in winter.

Fire destroys trash and waste materials.
It can even kill harmful germs.

But fire is not always useful.
It can be dangerous.
If you try to touch fire, you get burned.
Fire can destroy houses and forests.

Everyone needs fire.
But no one should use fire
unless he or she knows how.
When people are not careful, fire can be an enemy.
When people are careful, fire is a friend.

Born in Mount Vernon, Illinois, Gail Kay Haines
grew up in Paducah, Kentucky. An analytical chemist
and a member of the American Chemical Society,
she holds a degree in chemistry from Washington University,
in St. Louis, Missouri. Her first children's book
entitled *The Elements* was published in 1972.
At present, Mrs. Haines, her husband, and their two children,
a son and a daughter, live in Olympia, Washington.

Jacqueline Chwast was born in Newark, New Jersey,
and attended the Newark School of Fine and Industrial Arts.
The illustrator of seven children's books,
she has also written and illustrated two titles,
When the Baby Sitter Didn't Come and
How Mr. Berry Found a Home and Happiness Forever.
Mrs. Chwast lives in New York City with her two daughters.